I Am She

Eloise Newey

BookLeaf Publishing

Presentation by *BookLeaf Publishing*

Web: www.bookleafpub.com

E-mail: info@bookleafpub.com

ISBN: 9789357213578

First edition 2023

For Grandad, I miss you. And for Gareth.
Husband, best friend and biggest supporter.

Grandad

I dreamt of you last night
Saw your kind and smiling face
It made me think of memories
That no one can replace

Driving diggers and spiking punch
Fishing trips galore
Stories told upon your lap
From happy times to war

We'll miss your silly tricks
Like removing your false teeth
Press your nose and twist your ear
Helps us smile through the grief

Your children, grand and great
From the biggest to the small
Are lucky to have had you
For you loved us one and all

Now your suffering is over
For that we all are glad
But seeing your empty chair
Will always make us sad

Oh grandad how we'll miss you
Our loss is heavens gain
In our hearts you'll stay forever
Until we meet again

We call them Nurse

A battalion of soldiers
An army in blue
Taking fight without guns
For your family and you

Dressings and needles
Their weapons of choice
Hard working hands
Yet so soft of voice

Long hours they work
Some through night and day
Gentle and caring
Because that is their way

They weather the storms
For better for worse
Their names you know well
For we call them Nurse

I am She

She is running on empty
But still she shows up
She is bone tired
But still she smiles
She is self-loathing
But still she looks happy
She is often crying
But still she laughs
She is hurting
But still she helps others
She is crippled
But still she gets up
She is broken
But still she stands

I am She

Allotment Life

A small patch of scrubby land
Master plans abound
With buckets of enthusiasm
Begin digging up the ground

Pulling up the weeds and stones
Raking out the rough
Measuring for beds and runs
It never seems enough

Finally some planting
Lots of pots and tiny seeds
Watching, waiting, watering
Tending to their needs

Hardening off outside
Cursing late spring frosts
Transplant into the ground
Sad for those you lost

Now to watch them grow
Getting bigger by the day
Squashes, beans and corn
What an impressive display

When harvest time arrives
You pick it with great pride
Although some crops did fail
You gave your best and tried

Allotment life is hard
But the benefits are great
Reaping what you sow
As it ends up on your plate!

Final Day

Last day at primary has arrived
7 years have gone so fast
Sad to see an era end
But we knew it wouldn't last

You used to hold our hands
Give hugs when you came out
The biggest grin upon your face
"Mummy!" you would shout

The smiles and hugs got less
Your independence grown
No longer need a hand to hold
You can walk to school alone

A fresh chapter awaits now
A new school to start
As calm as you may feel
I know you'll be sad to depart

So enjoy your final day
Making memories to treasure
And a long summer ahead
That will stay with you forever

For a young man you're becoming
It makes us proud to see
Not a baby anymore
But our first born you'll always be

Drowning

Too many emotions
Swirling shades of grey
Feeling like I'm drowning
Struggling day to day

An onslaught of calls
Some unrealistic demands
A host of unhappy patients
Giving out reprimands

We're smiling through the pain
Yet crying silently inside
Running ourselves down
For this service we provide

For while we may help others
Our own health does suffer
Somethings bound to give
If we don't soon get tougher

So know that we are here
Ready to take your call
Dealing with all problems
From the biggest to the small

But treat us with the care
That you in turn do crave
For we are human too
And all we had we gave

My Love

You called for me last night my love
At two then three then four
Your crying like a siren
That my brain cannot ignore

Though my body's very tired
And I long to stay in bed
I made a promise to you
So here I am instead

It may be just a hug you need
Or a word into your ear
The gentle reassurance
Knowing somebody is here

For you are only small my love
The nights are dark and long
Shout and I will find you
To soothe you with a song

Your body warm on mine
Snuggled up against my chest
Little sobs receding
As you settle back to rest

I know as you get older
You'll need me less and less
Though sometimes I may grumble
I will miss this, I confess

But I'll always be here my love
Even when you're big and grown
Because I am your mother
And where I am is home

Global Pandemic

A global pandemic
Brought all to their knees
A world kept apart
By a deadly disease

Daily life was shut down
Not a moment too soon
As keyworkers rose up
A small light in the gloom

We all pulled together
Though apart we remained
Trying our hardest
To keep the virus contained

Loved ones were lost
Released from their bind
But no hugs or comfort
For those left behind

We clapped for our heroes
Drew rainbows galore
Though soon we grew restless
And started to bore

Tired of being constrained
Complacent we became
Relaxing the rules
But much to our shame

The virus mutated
Infecting more by the day
Suitable punishment
For being led astray

The NHS buckled
And bent under strain
Yet staff still attended
Time and again

Then a glimmer of hope
A vaccine approved
A light in the dark
Things may yet improve

Giant hubs were set up
A mass of man power
Injecting the world
Hour upon hour

We're tired and broken
But won't stop the fight
One last big push
The end is in sight

So keep your chin up
Aim for victory
One thing's for sure
We're making history!

For Kate

If truly there's a time to go
Then yours has come too soon
Such brief a time upon this Earth
You danced to your own tune

Happy smiling eyes
Your face split with a grin
Silly hats upon your head
Happy Fridays at the Inn

Tents and music festivals
Daily antics with the cat
A ready ear for listening
Or popping for a chat

Kindness beyond measure
Happiness you did provide
For all your friends and family
Especially your husband Clive

All these precious memories
When we see or speak your name
Will all come flooding back
And we'll remember you again

You'll never be forgotten
For even though you may be gone
Your tune it stays behind and
In people's hearts you will live on

Librarian

Come inside and take a peek
Tell us what it is you seek

Don't be afraid of our looks
Row upon row of dusty books

We can offer reason or rhyme
Pop and have some quiet time

Curled up in a cosy chair
No one will disturb you there

Not as scary as we seem
Giving you the chance to dream

Masters of the printed word
Help release your inner nerd

All of this and it is free
Librarians by nature are we

What Christmas means to me

Twinkling lights and baubles
Presents under the tree
Advent chocs for breakfast
Mince pies and cream for tea

Naughty elves at play
A wreath upon your door
Wearing festive jumpers
Wrapping paper on the floor

Attending midnight mass
Carols being sung
A home to decorate
And garlands to be hung

Day trip to see Santa
Reindeer food to make
A nativity to watch
Then back in time to bake

Families get together
A table neatly laid
Food and drink aplenty
Board games to be played

It's a magical time of year
I think we can agree
All these things and more
Are what Christmas means to me

Nature's Dance

The changing of the seasons
A joyous sight to see
I can take you on a journey
Take my hand and come with me

Winter months seem bleak
But there's pleasure to be found
In dark nights snuggled up and
White snow upon the ground

Spring it brings new hope
Green buds, new leaves and shoots
The yellow sun feels stronger
Warming soil for new roots

Summer gives us longer days
Aquamarine blue skies
Golden sand and ice creams
Watching the sunset and sunrise

Autumn is my favourite
Leaves change before your eyes
Orange, browns and reds
As the foliage slowly dies

It's a myriad of colours
A full spectrum in play
As nature does her dance
Bringing joy along the way

Take a break

I have battled with dragons
And ridden a broom
Danced with the fairies
Stroked a Phoenix's plume

I have joined an army
Fought with a sword
Met Kings and Queens
Fell in love with a Lord

I have walked with giants
Flown a rocket to space
Ran away with the circus
And solved a mystery case

I have swam with a whale
Conversed with the trees
Lived deep underground
And sailed the seas

I have lived many lives
Visited many a shore
"But how is this possible?"
I hear you implore

The answer is simple
Should you care to look
Take a break from this world
And pick up a book!

Bring you back

Feeling so hopeless
Life begins to unfold
Unable to go on
Sadness takes hold

Dark thoughts swirling
Lost in your head
Considering the worst
While alone in your bed

Believing the words
From deep in your mind
Without considerations
For those left behind

It's hard to think straight
Your insides twist and bend
Desperation takes over
You want this to end

There on the edge
In the dead of night
A knowing sensation
"This isn't right"

You bravely reach out
Take a different leap
From the one you had planned
When lacking in sleep

A listening ear
With a warm embrace
A hand to hold
In a comforting place

Though it's still hard
Know you're not alone
We're all here for you
At the end of a phone

One step at a time
We'll help you cope
To bring you back
And be your hope

Husband and Wife

Come dance with me
In to the storm
Hold on tight
I'll keep you warm

Follow me there
To the rainbows end
Where treasure awaits
For us my friend

Let's walk this path
Stay side by side
You be my light
I'll be your guide

Along ups and downs
We twist and we turn
Make mistakes on the way
There's lots to learn

We move with grace
Though sometimes stumble
Our bond is strong
We'll never crumble

A great team we make
As we navigate life
For you are my husband
And I am your wife

Soothe Your Soul

The sound of crashing waves
Soft sand between your toes
Warm sun upon your face
Can chase away your woes

The smell of fresh cut grass
Trees swaying in the breeze
A river flowing fast and free
Help put your mind at ease

A canopy of branches
Twigs snapping as you stroll
The sound of birdsong in the air
Are soothing for your soul

So invest in some self care
Step away from the daily grind
To enjoy the things around you
Relax, de-stress and unwind

A Blanket of White

Huge, soft goose feathers
Falling silent from the sky
Gently swirling to the ground
A pleasure to the eye

Blanketing the world in white
Picture perfect as a card
Catching snowflakes in your hand
Children playing out in the yard

Snowmen of all sizes
Noses starting to chill
Laughter ringing in the air
From sledders on the hill

All too soon it starts to melt
White turning in to grey
The world returned to normal
Until the next snow day

The last goodbye

All things heal with time
At least that's what they say
Months march on to years
Hours turn in to days

Although the pain it lessens
I learned to live with grief
It makes it no less easier
The time it felt too brief

I held your hand in mine
Stayed close to your bedside
Crying while my heart broke
As the light inside you died

The last goodbye was hard
It's etched into my mind
Words are little comfort
For those that are left behind

I keep on moving forward
Through the sadness and the pain
But I carry you within my heart
And with me you'll remain

Sweet tooth

Lemon loaf and Pecan pie
These are things that catch my eye

Rocky road and brownies too
These things I can share with you

Ginger nuts and chocolate mousse
Can be used to call a truce

Vicky sponge and small cupcakes
These are things my mother bakes

Macaroons and jam swiss roll
These are soothing for the soul

Cake or biscuit any will do
Have you got a sweet tooth too?

International Nurses Day

Battered and bent
From this battle they fight
Running on empty
Doing what's right

Though fragile in state
They stand proud and tall
Living this nightmare
Still giving their all

They put you and yours
Above any of their own
The last ones to leave
And the first to have shown

So give them a smile
Treat them with respect
The small courtesies
That you would expect

They do this for you
This job they adore
A strong dedication
You cannot ignore

Recognition we give
For this role so diverse
Shout loud from the rooftop
WE THANK YOU NURSE!

My world

The moment that I saw you
I knew you were for me
You lit a spark inside
That was clear for all to see

You made my tummy tumble
Set my heart to racing fast
You liked my pixie hair
Didn't care about my past

You took me as I was
Tomboy clothes and all
I often sat and wondered
Why you returned my call

You showed me how to love
And shared your future plans
Wrapped your arms around me
Held my world in your hands

I had little to give in return
But my heart I gave to you
Many years before the day
We said the words "I do"

Now I couldn't be without you
Fate came just in time
I'll be forever yours my love
And you'll always be mine

www.ingramcontent.com/pod-product-compliance
Lightning Source LLC
Chambersburg PA
CBHW051747130826
49812CB00033B/1039
9789357213578